HIGH
SALES MANAGEMENT

Elaine and John Frazer-Robinson

60 Minutes Success Skills Series

Copyright © John Frazer-Robinson 1999

First published 1999 by
David Grant Publishing Limited
80 Ridgeway
Pembury
Kent TN2 4EZ
United Kingdom

01   00   99   10 9 8 7 6 5 4 3 2 1

60 Minutes Success Skills Series is an imprint of
David Grant Publishing Limited

All rights reserved. Except for the quotation of short passages for the purposes of criticism and review, no part of this publication may be reproduced, stored in a retrieval system, or transmitted, in any form or by any means, electronic, mechanical, photocopying, recording or otherwise, without the prior permission of the publisher.

British Library Cataloguing in Publication Data
A CIP catalogue record for this book is available from the British Library

ISBN 1-901306-26-7

Cover design: Liz Rowe
Text design: Graham Rich
Production coordinator: Paul Stringer
Edited and Typeset in Futura by Kate Williams
Printed and bound in Great Britain by
T.J. International Ltd, Padstow, Cornwall

This book is printed on acid-free paper

The publishers accept no responsibility for any investment or financial decisions made on the basis of the information in this book. Readers are advised always to consult a qualified financial adviser.

All names mentioned in the text have been changed to protect the identity of the business people involved. Any resemblance to existing companies or people is entirely coincidental.

Contents

Welcome: About *High Perfomance Sales Management*   5

Chapter 1: The Customer Is King   7
    Customer focus
    The Golden Rule of 75
    What kind of team do you want to manage?
    Customer relationship skills
    The 'as others see you' exercise

Chapter 2: Making Time for Your Team   13
    Managing your time
    What is teamwork?
    Five key issues for planning
    Creating a sales plan
    Information, objectives, strategies, action and timing

Chapter 3: The Secrets of Motivating your Team   23
    Mastering motivation and 3D motivation
    Why money can't buy you love!
    What motivates people
    Self-motivation exercises
    Developing clarity of task
    Living with IMPs!

Chapter 4: Using Performance to Create Winners   31
    OUTcomes and INfluences
    Working with Customers
    The value of regular visits
    Building rapport skills
    Prioritising activity
    Goal setting

Chapter 5: The Secrets of Coaching and Training   41
   The four stages of learning
   Becoming unnecessary – but vital!
   Training and coaching methods and topics
   Giving and receiving feedback
   Accompanied visits
   How to become a great leader

Chapter 6: Running Great Sales Team Meetings   51
   Where to get help
   Beginnings, middles and ends
   A CLEAR formula for successful meetings
   Before you meet
   Checklist for great meetings

Chapter 7: Ready for Lift-off   57
   If you go on doing . . .
   Get ready now!
   Celebrate your power
   An open door to success

WELCOME!

ABOUT *HIGH PERFORMANCE SALES MANAGEMENT*

Whether you are a seasoned sales manager, an aspiring sales manager or employed anywhere in sales, marketing or elsewhere in business, *High Performance Sales Management* will teach you all you need to know about the role of today's sales manager. Note that the most important word in the last sentence was "today's".

In an increasingly competitive world, it is vital not just to satisfy your Customers but to create a mutually beneficial relationship with them. This book will give you the tools with which to do so.

How does this book work?

To begin with, settle yourself somewhere quiet and comfortable and read the entire book. Next, use the book for reference – when you need some help, glance through it to remind yourself of all the various ideas and tips. Lastly, refresh your ideas by using the book on an ongoing basis. For instance, why not re-read a chapter each month until you feel you've absorbed it totally?

About the 60 Minutes series

The 60 Minutes Success Skills Series is written for people with neither the time nor the patience to trawl through acres of jargon, management-speak and page-filling waffle. Like all the books in the series, *High Performance Sales Management* has been written in the belief that you can learn all you really need to know quickly and without hassle. The aim is to distil the essential, practical advice you can use straight away.

Good luck!

THE CUSTOMER IS KING

Chapter 1

Coming up in this chapter

Customer focus
The Golden Rule of 75
What kind of team do you want to manage?
Customer relationship skills
The 'as others see you' exercise

In the past few years the role of the sales manager has changed radically. Indeed, businesses have changed radically, but perhaps no more so than in sales and marketing. Around the world, after 30 years of rhetoric and fine words, the Customer is becoming king. And this, therefore, must be the premise from which we start our journey together. A few years back we wrote:

> *The object of a business is NOT to make money.*
> *The object of a business is to satisfy its Customers.*
> *The* result *is to make money*

The Five Rules of 75

In this book we will introduce you to the Five Rules of 75. These rules address the five fundamental principles that hold the key to the effectiveness of the team and your prowess at managing them. They concern the share of Customer spend you achieve; the amount of your time spent with your team; the priority you give to motivating your team; how you use team meetings; and where you focus team sales activity. They will be explained in detail. Let them lead you to high performance.

The Customer should be the first and most important priority for any business. On this topic, we admit, we do have our quirks and eccentricities. For example, we prefer to ban "military language" from sales and marketing. And we always spell Customer with a capital C!

Over the years the twinned worlds of sales and marketing became obsessed with transactions rather than relationships;

obsessed with the next sale. As an industry, we forgot one of the oldest maxims in the selling world:

> **"** *When the sale takes precedence over my relationship with my Customers, I can tell you what has happened. My next sale has lost out to this one!* **"**
> **– Heinz Goldman, The Art of Selling, 1966**

It is always easier to repeat sell to an existing Customer than to anyone else. Typical figures suggest that it is at least five times easier. Our experience suggests that it is often nearer 15 times easier!

The lesson is simple. Shift the focus, time and effort of your team on to the under-nourished existing Customers. Serve them fully. Treat them with respect and courtesy. Do everything in your power to understand their needs. Meet those needs. Consciously work to build your share of the available and appropriate 'wallet' for that family, household or business, and suddenly the whole picture is transformed. There shouldn't be a single Customer out there who is not receiving regular reviews, visits and calls.

If most businesses had anything like 75% of the available spend of its Customers, annual targets would be met in the first month. Most businesses neglect Customers and, as a result, Customers place business elsewhere.

'Available spend', for a business, would probably be a budget. For a consumer, it is their appropriate, affordable or desired amount. Often this is a notional assessment but you can easily ask the Customer.

So let's engrave the Golden Rule of 75 into our hearts and minds.

The Golden Rule of 75

When you have captured at least 75% of the Customers' available spend, you know you have secured their trust, their loyalty and their affection.

THE CUSTOMER IS KING

Attaining this level of saturation of your team's Customer base will probably remain a dream. However, reach for it. There is no faster way for your team to smash through their targets!

> Smart sales management is about educating and encouraging team members to appreciate the value of regular Customer reviews, skilled and sensitive referral-seeking and frequent Customer contact.
> Salespeople should be encouraged to build activity across all these tasks and to discuss and share their successes and failures with their team colleagues at regular sales meetings. Whatever it is that your business sells, make it a goal to, in the nicest possible way, 'own' that Customer. Make sure you get at least 75% of their business.

What kind of team do you want to manage?

Modern sales management operates most effectively in a regime of openness, support and encouragement. The sales manager should both show these qualities and expect them from the team members. This requires a mature attitude to the management task; an attitude which is open to the responsibility of achievement as well as understanding the support required by the individuals who make up the team.

When you engender feelings of empowerment and responsibility within your team, they have to learn how to handle it. It's a mutual growth process. Some managers won't make it. They will be too stuck in the old methods to let go. Some sales people also won't respond to this culture. Their idea of strong leadership is different. They're stuck in what they see as "the good old days".

Your team culture should see ignorance as the opportunity to learn, and failure as an opportunity to succeed. Your culture should welcome those who say, "Tell me more; I'd like to learn that". Make no mistake, businesses cannot tolerate ignorance and failure. Life is too tough, too competitive, to carry those who don't, or won't, learn. Growth carries responsibility for the individuals as well as the team leader.

The future is better . . . but harder

Nowadays, senior management is looking for enterprise and initiative from its stars. They appreciate that you and your team are out there with the Customers. You see, hear and feel Customer needs. It is in assisting your team to meet those needs that you and your management can best achieve the aims of the business.

Customer-driven selling – the way to high performance

You may have been a sales manager for some years, and it would be very easy to sit back and say, "I'm OK. I've been a manager quite a while. I know how to do it. I don't need this book." But take that risk at your peril, for in the Customer-focused ethos the task and role of the sales manager is different. You have explicit objectives to deliver a quality-based, service-orientated method of gaining sales, which is arrived at by making the vehicle for sales achievement a strong, caring and satisfying Customer relationship. Today's sales manager is predominantly a coach and trainer. There's an emotional and psychological content to your work.

> Seek out the salespeople who want to grow with you. Nurture those who welcome their new found skills and who participate and involve themselves in the learning process. Honour those who work with a team spirit and commitment. These are tomorrow's winners. They not only need to sell, they need to sell well. Anything less and you have a problem.

How do you learn Customer relationship skills?

Discuss this with your team. Seek out people you admire and talk to them. Observe and learn. Bury yourself in books and hunt down videos. There's plenty available on rapport-building, the art of listening, questioning techniques, and so on. Discuss with your manager how you can experiment with new ways and seek his or her participation and involvement.

Remember, your task is to cultivate and enable your team. Your manager's task is to cultivate and enable you. But you must demonstrably join in and take initiatives, just as you should expect your team members to do the same. If your manager doesn't respond, don't give up! Find a peer and work together to support each other.

Most of your work will be an interaction of one sort or another with your sales people. So start your development process by actually considering your management style and why you use that style. Establish what exactly are the skills and competences of a sales manager and a sales person, and review yourself and your team members against these.

> **Getting to know yourself as a manager**
>
> Write down a description of yourself. List your personal strengths and weaknesses. Describe your team members too. Examine why you get on better with some members than others. Is it their personality type that dictates how you work with them, or is it yours? Personality types are deeply embedded in us (thanks to the influence of Mum, Dad and a few others!). You are unlikely to want or be able to change your essential personality – that's you! – and you must not expect your team members to change theirs.
>
> However, with consideration, you can start to understand why, when you do things differently, they respond differently. Modifying a personality is difficult; modifying a behaviour is also difficult, but it is the easier and more productive of the two!

When you feel you and they are ready for it, get your team members to carry out the first exercise above. Let them describe themselves, then similarly describe you. You should do likewise, and then compare notes. Do it on a one-to-one basis. As well as creating a bridge between the two of you, you will begin to realise how different your perceptions are of each other and where you chafe. Laugh and have fun. Discuss together how you can both modify your behaviour towards each other, then you can improve how you work together.

HIGH PERFORMANCE SALES MANAGEMENT

Wanting to learn is not a sign of weakness or inadequacy. You are showing yourself to be ready, willing and able. Just as you must create safety for your team members to display their weaknesses, to seek your support and help, so you too have the same right to respect from your peer group and manager. If you don't get it, SHOUT. If your manager doesn't respond, find a peer and support each other.

1. When the sales takes precedence over the relationship with Customers, the second sale has lost out to the first.
2. It is 5–15 times easier to obtain repeat business from an existing Customer than to find new business.
3. Treat Customers with respect and courtesy. Do everything in your power to understand their needs. Meet those needs. Consciously work to build your share of the available or appropriate "wallet" for that family, household or business.
4. The Golden Rule of 75: *When you have captured at least 75% of the Customers' available spend, you know you have secured their trust, loyalty and affection.*
5. Your task is to cultivate and enable your team. Your manager's task is to cultivate and enable you.

MAKING TIME FOR YOUR TEAM — Chapter 2

Coming up in this chapter

Managing your time
What is teamwork?
Five key issues for planning
Creating a sales plan
Information, objectives, strategies, action and timing

Your task as a manager is to develop your team to enable them to coast to their targets themselves, knowing that you, their manager, are constantly supporting them, improving their selling skills, fine tuning their product knowledge and Customer service capabilities and helping them to succeed in a changing and competitive environment. That will feel like real management. It demonstrates trust in them and care for them. It empowers them to do their job with confidence and capability. It benefits all concerned.

The Rule of 75 and effective management

What is the essential difference between a run-of-the-mill sales manager and a high performance sales manager? The answer is usually clear for all to see. The run-of-the-mill manager is busy doing things; the high performance manager is busy managing. In fact, such a truly high performance manager has probably already learned the Time Rule of 75. This is a simple rule.

> **The Time Rule of 75**
>
> Organise your time and activities to enable you to spend 75% of your time out with your team.   **RULE**

Let's call that "teamtime". When you achieve this level of teamtime commitment to your sales people, then you know they, and you, have the best chance of hitting targets. In other words, you will at least have arrived in the high performance zone.

Examine how you spend your time

In order to discover how you might achieve this 75% teamtime, you must examine how you spend your time at present. For many the realisation that their time should be managed and quite determinedly allocated is a major breakthrough.

Sales managers who analyse their time are often daunted by the gap between where they are and where they want to be. Don't panic if this is also true for you. The fact is that getting to 75% requires altering the way you do things as well as what you do. That is to say, you can gain extra teamtime by changing the way you carry out some of your management or administration tasks.

Sales people must be active. If they are well managed, they become more active and sell more. Sales managers, on the other hand, must manage. Their pure selling activity should be as near zero as possible. The nearer they can get to zero, the nearer they can get to the Time Rule of 75.

Low-performance managers busy themselves with everything but being with their teams. This is a definite sign of managers who do not understand the dynamics of high performance. They may even lack the confidence to manage and therefore spend much of their time in the comfortable pursuit of doing what they perceive they do best – selling, for example!

Redefine your work

High performance sales managers only accept these two categories of work: "teamwork" covers anything to do with people or their tasks and "officework" covers the remainder. Therefore, the Rule of 75 is that all teamtime is made up of teamwork. Officework is confined to, at most, the remaining 25%.

The words *teamwork* and *officework* should not be taken literally. Tasks that are categorised as officework could be done in a hotel room, not necessarily at your desk in the office.

Those who want to achieve the Time Rule of 75 do so because they understand that this portion of their life is about their team as individuals and as a whole. This time – teamtime – has the highest leverage and the highest payback potential of all. This is where the high performance manager can make the BIG difference. Therefore, "officework" tasks, as essential as they are, must be kept to a minimum and must be allocated the shortest time.

Consider the teamwork activities below, starting with those that, while essential, should be the least demanding on your time.

Appraisals
There are two kinds of appraisal: formal and informal. Many companies operate an annual formal appraisal system and everyone falls in with it, failing to realise just how powerful appraisals can be to building motivation, identifying development needs and improving performance.

Informal appraisals will be those that you carry out more regularly among your team. High performance sales managers carry out informal appraisals with their team members at least quarterly and, if there should be difficulties or problems, more frequently still. Try to avoid lumping all the appraisals together. Spread them evenly over the month and you'll find that your appraisals are of a much better quality.

In your appraisals:
- ❑ concentrate on the difference you can make to the future, and don't get bogged down with the past;
- ❑ understand that appraisals are about analysis and development of your team members' skills and competences;
- ❑ praise generously as well as discussing the improvements you want;
- ❑ together ensure you end up with a personal development plan;
- ❑ specify the next appraisal date and what your expectations are by that date

Sales analysis and planning
This involves goal setting and action planning individually and with your team. It's a good subject for individual reviews and teamwork. And it's a good use of teamtime. Sales people are

much more likely to deliver to expectations they have helped to create rather than to those that have been handed to them. Review these very regularly – at least monthly – with individuals and as a team. You'll find more about sales plans on page 19.

Sales planning should include the number of visits and telephone calls – including existing Customers and prospecting calls – and how these will be achieved to meet their agreed annual and monthly targets. It should also show the coaching and training required and when it should take place. Be specific and precise.

There should be a direct link between sales plans and the development plans that result from the appraisals.

Team communications
Spoken and written communications with your team – whether by phone, letter, fax, e-mail or in person – are vital for giving team members their personal recognition and for building team spirit. Spend at least one day a month working on your own communication skills as well as on improving the communications to which you are applying them.

Make sure your team are constantly amazed by the way you are always there for them and interested in what they are doing. If you have the slightest element of "control freak" in you, work hard to bury it deep at these moments!

Sales team meetings
These form a major tool for the high performance sales manager. They are the principal forum for team building and play an important part in developing and maintaining team morale and individual motivation. Devote at least two full days a month to this activity and your team will feel the benefit of their teamtime. You'll find this book is full of ideas that can be used well in team meetings, and there is a chapter devoted to this important subject.

Development through training and coaching

Giving support, help and understanding to team members individually will build enthusiasm and loyalty and they will equally be certain of your dedication to their personal welfare, growth and success. Of all the time you spend with your team, either individually or as a group, that spent coaching is by far the most important. Coaching is an activity in which you must become expert. A good deal of your coaching will involve accompanied sales visits, which need meticulous planning. You'll find more on this and some preparation checklists in the chapter on training and coaching.

> Be sure to push your own line managers to train you and help you to develop your skills. Push hardest for things that will help you build your coaching and leadership skills. It is in these skills where the most leverage for success and growth exists.

What are the qualities of a good salesperson?

Observe your team and others inside and outside the company. See if you can spot the difference between the most successful sales people and the rest. When you identify differences, bring them up for discussion at meetings. Spread skills among your team and don't hesitate to involve your team members in this process or to ask other company people to address your team members about what they have found works for them.

If you nurture and develop your team members and ensure that you devote yourself to plenty of coaching and training, then you have taken a really important step to high performance sales management. You'll also be operating in the perfect environment: you'll have achieved the Time Rule of 75.

The four key 'ownership' issues

All sales teams need to understand and share ownership of their goals in relation to four key issues:

1. Where are you now?
(Analysis of results and sales activity and management data)

With sales results analysis and activity and other management data you have diagnostic tools for learning. You also have a vehicle that has a great set of hazard warning lights. Use graphs to watch trends and you will be able to nip disasters in the bud and keep the team on track. In these figures lie your early warning systems. Positive trends can be just as interesting; look to see if someone has either found a new technique or idea or, even, a new reason for Customers or prospects to buy. From a team point of view, graphs can be very telling because they give you a clear picture of any gap between achievement and target.

> **The top eleven performance measures**
> - Conversion rate from enquiry to proposal
> - Closing rate from proposal to sale
> - Average order values
> - Selling across the product range (cross-selling)
> - Repeat sales to existing Customers (up-selling)
> - Proportion of sales to existing Customers against new Customers
> - Sales per week/hour/day
> - Sales to cost ratio
> - Second sales to new Customers
> - Customer longevity
> - Complaint levels

It is vital to discuss this analysis with the individual in question or, when dealing with team results, the whole team. If you are to breed a sufficiently strong team spirit, ownership of goals, successes and failures is absolutely crucial.

2. Where do you want to be?
(Sales targets, manning and performance planning)

Once your analysis and examination of results are complete, you can look at the remainder of the period, regardless of whether it is a whole or portion of a year, or simply the month ahead. What do you have to achieve, not just in sales but in all performance, skills and competence issues? This must be looked at from an individual and team perspective.

3. How do you get from one to the other?
(Assessment and appraisal of the gap plus a realistic path to where you want to be)

Let's just think about sales plans before we move to the gap analysis.

The sales plan
Sales plans have a nasty habit of being all important until they have been signed off by the individual, team, regional and national management. They are then filed for another year – generally at the bottom of a drawer!

A sales plan is a clear, achievable, measurable set of development objectives and actions that enable individuals to reach their agreed sales targets. Each member of your team should have an annual and monthly sales plan, which you and the member create together. The whole collection should match your team plan.

Sales plans must be flexible, as you will regularly review them and adapt them to market situations, amend them for further action and include additional training and coaching. It is best to have a common format for sales plans and keep them brief. Be time specific. Know where you have to be at a certain stage. Sales plans are easy. In fact, the shorter and simpler they are, the better they work.

If it is necessary for you to vary the plan or change tack, do it. But involve the individual concerned or your team in the reasoning and be sure to let them be creative in the ideas, actions and activities that you plan. By how much do you have to pump up activity? And how will this be achieved? What performance ratios need your coaching and training attention? Again, to gain commitment and enthusiasm, ownership of the resulting action plans must be shared between you and the sales person or you and the team, as appropriate.

You may not need to change the whole of your plan at each individual review or team meeting. Simple modifications may be enough. This checklist shows you how to analyse the gap and amend your plan.

Analysing the gap (data collection, objectives and strategies)

Information

Note trends by product, market and area. Include the results for the period and an overview of what is happening based on your summary of progress (or lack of it) with personal development. This should be done individually and by team.

Look at the sales you have made against the sales you thought you would make. Work out why that is. Look at the product mix sold, and the revenue you have achieved or not achieved. Check margins and profit contributions. Examine the difference between your expectation and what really happened. Examine what your competitors are doing and, every so often, review the SWOT analysis from the previous meeting to see if anything has moved or changed. (If you're not familiar with SWOT, see page 47.)

Objectives

Look at what the objectives were last time against the annual targets. Review how you've done and then look at what you have still to do. If you are doing well, don't sit back satisfied. High performance management is about exceeding goals – urge your team on to greater things. Move the boundaries further.

Strategies

What are the latest thoughts on how the business, region and area are doing? What effect does this have on your team's strategy for the rest of the year? How will you exceed target? When, where and why must you do the things that will enable you to get beyond your goals and what are those things?

Closing the gap (amendment of sales plan)

Once you have analysed the results the next step is to determine what you need to do to achieve targets and then amend the sales plan, if necessary.

Actions

Calculate the key performance indicators that will enable you to reach your goals. Pay particular attention to activity levels. Consider the selling methods you are using. Create action plans. Cover training and coaching activities. Review any activity, promotions or events that are forthcoming.

MAKING TIME FOR YOUR TEAM

Timing
Use the sales plan regularly to check back and forward and religiously monitor and review individual's and your team's progress.

4. How will you know you are there?
(Activity and competence monitoring and management)

Apart from the statistics telling you that you are there, and your graphs being proudly shown around, you will feel it! There will probably be a satisfied grin on your face and your team will be looking for congratulations and flattery! Hopefully, too, senior people will be ringing you with verbal "pats on the back".

However, performance improvement and individual development are never-ending processes. Figures should never go backwards and, equally, should never stop climbing. Standing still is losing ground in the battle to serve the Customer better. There is always something you can do to improve. Even with your best people, you should expect constant growth and evolution. Next quarter's targets should be higher than this quarter's. Next year's targets should be higher than this year's. Growth, development and improvement must be seen, felt and recognised and give tangible, real results.

It is your task as a high performance manager to use the activity planning functions of your job for the positive benefit of your team. When you use them with involvement, you create a clear set of tasks. When you create clear tasks, people know what to do. When people know what to do they feel capable and empowered. This links to motivation and enthusiasm. Motivated and enthusiastic people become determined to succeed. They can smell success. They want to win – for themselves and for the team. Light their fire!

> 1. **Redefine your work. Find ways to motivate, coach and encourage your team members, transforming everyday work into valuable teamtime. Avoid wasting your time selling – spend all your time helping the team to sell better for you.**
> 2. **The Time Rule of 75:** *spend 75% of your time out with your team.*

3. Every sales team needs to understand and share ownership of its goals in relation to four key issues: analysis of results and sales activity and management data; assessment and appraisal of any gap or deficiency combined with realistic forecasting; sales planning; activity and competence monitoring.
4. A sales plan is a clear, achievable, measurable set of objectives and actions that will take you from your present position to where you want to be by the end of the period in question. Sales plans should contain team members' figures to match the results you need.
5. Sales plans should include sales and market information, objectives, strategies, actions and timing.

The Secrets of Motivating Your Team — Chapter 3

Coming up in this chapter

Mastering motivation and 3D motivation
Why money can't buy you love!
What motivates people
Self-motivation exercises
Developing clarity of task
Living with IMPs!

Become a master of motivation

An effective sales manager takes the time and makes the effort to become a master of motivation. The first secret of motivation is that you cannot motivate others if you are not motivated yourself. You will find that motivation has three dimensions – self, team members and team – just as personal relationships have me, you and us. And just as all three dimensions of the personal relationship need time, attention and work, so do the three dimensions of sales motivation.

> You have not only to ensure that your team is motivated, you have also to make sure that your manager is paying enough attention to your motivation. If you don't feel you are receiving enough attention – remember, SHOUT. And shout loudly. No one can over emphasise the need for abundant motivation in the sales force. All sales managers must take this responsibility very seriously, both in terms of what they give and what they receive.

So here is the next Rule of 75. It's the Focus Rule of 75.

> **The Focus Rule of 75**
>
> Of all the time that you spend with your team 75% of it must be spent on motivation.

twenty-three

What is motivation?

The dictionary definition of motivation is, "The action or an act of motivating something or someone". That's a bit obvious! But it does go on to be a little more helpful with this: "The conscious or unconscious stimulus, incentive or motive, etc. for action towards a goal especially resulting from psychological or social factors; the factors giving purpose or direction to the behaviour". That's a little nearer what's needed. However, and for the purpose of this chapter, let's write our own definition. Motivation is getting people, cheerfully, willingly and professionally to do the things that will meet the business's goals and objectives.

What motivates people?

Managers should have, in their job descriptions, responsibility for the motivation of their staff. But where do you start? Many see it as whipcracking their team into action; some view the task as if they were in the police force; others as a legitimised form of bullying.

Over the past 30 or so years a great deal of work has been done on trying to understand human motivation. Maslow's hierarchy of human needs suggests three sets of human needs.

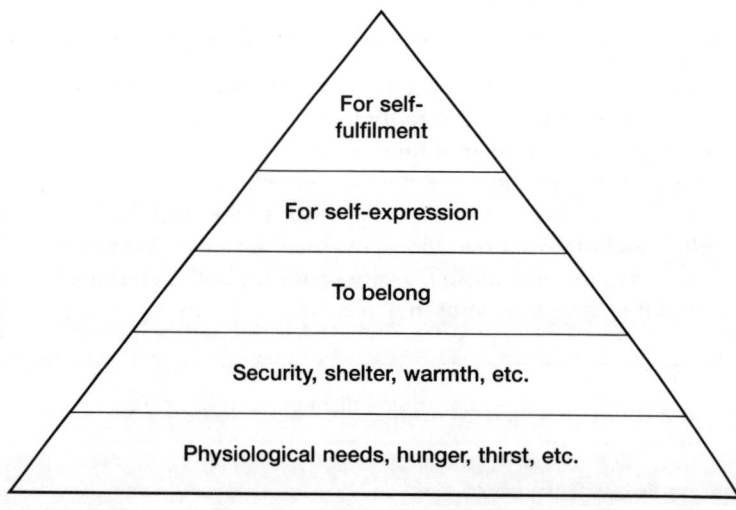

Maslow's hierarchy of human needs (Source: Abraham H. Maslow, *Motivation and Personality*, Copyright 1954 Harper & Row Inc. Reprinted by permission of HarperCollins Publishers)

The theory is that as each set of needs was met, so the next level of needs established itself. As our bodily needs for food and water were met, we then craved security, shelter and warmth. Given these, our next need was to belong. If we felt we belonged, then we searched for self-expression and finally – if we could express ourselves – self-fulfilment became the priority. Our motivational work places its major emphasis on the top three layers of Maslow's hierarchy: *belonging* (this is why teams ultimately bring out more of an individual's performance), *self-expression* and *self-fulfilment*.

> **Gimme Money!**
>
> It surprises many that salary and commission fall in the two bottom layers (security and physiological needs). But consider why people might descend the hierarchy as well as why they climb it. Consider, for example, money. In connection with motivation, money becomes far more of an issue when the top three layers of the hierarchy (belonging, self-expression and self-fulfilment) are deficient or failing. Money is only an issue with teams of low or no motivation. Remember, if you are achieving your targets, you will be rewarded. Money is no longer the issue
> It is almost as though, when one of our layers is taken away – or that level of needs is not met – we compensate on the layer below. If that isn't strong enough we continue to descend to a level we find comfortable and wallow around in that level, compensating ourselves with extra need gratification.

Why incentives or money are not the right solution

Many cash-based incentives and holiday competitions have been badly discredited and demonstrated poor and short-term effects on sales. Also, in terms of being Customer-driven, they tend to drive things over Customers rather than for them!

But who wins with cash prizes, incentives and competitions? Only the winners . . . and certainly not the Customer. Incentives like these only really boost performance from those who think they have a chance; those who least need incentives in the first place. The result is a short-term boost in sales that, for motivation building, usually does nothing that has any prolonged effect on the whole sales force. These categories of motivator have no sustained effect on motivation, fail to work for the vast majority of the team and leave behind a trail of Customers who were sold to for the wrong reasons: the seller's reasons, not the Customer's. Moreover they work against team spirit, driving individuals to put their own interests first.

> High performance sales managers should concentrate on the three upper ranges of needs where they will have the greatest success. Here lie such needs as achievement and accomplishment. Remember, these are the need to *belong*, the need for *self-expression* and the need for *self-fulfillment*. Concentrate on these. Members of a motivated team hit their targets so the financial rewards follow anyway.

How can motivation improve sales performance?

The task of the manager is to create the environment and conditions in which self-motivation will flourish and grow. McGregor sought to demonstrate this with his landmark work The XY Theory. Originally published in 1960, it is only recently that its relevance has become more widely understood, acknowledged and appreciated.

X and Y represent two different extremes of treating people. From the McGregor's XY theory table opposite, you will recognise X as the "old fashioned" way and Y as the "enlightened" way. If you treat people as in belief system X they will react accordingly. They will need to be carefully watched with strict rules, tight discipline and bonus and incentives regularly applied.

X people are highly unmotivated, largely unhappy and often rebellious. They find work a chore, feel that their creativity is unwanted and undervalued, that they have no voice and that the system is there to make them obey the rules.

THE SECRETS OF MOTIVATING YOUR TEAM

McGregor's XY theory (from *The Human Side of Enterprise*, McGraw-Hill, 1960)

The X group	The Y group
1 People dislike work and will avoid it if they can	1 Work is necessary to people's psychological growth
2 People must be forced or bribed to put out the right effort	2 People want to be interested in their work and, under the right conditions, they can enjoy it
3 People would rather be directed than accept responsibility, which they avoid	3 People will direct themselves towards an accepted target
	4 People will seek, and accept, responsibility under the right conditions
	5 The discipline people impose on themselves is more effective, and can be more severe, than any imposed on them
4 People are motivated mainly by money	6 Under the right conditions people are motivated by the desire to realise their own potential
5 People are motivated by their anxiety about their security	
6 Most people have little creativity – except when getting round management rules	7 Creativity and ingenuity are widely distributed and grossly under-used

Y people will be sales people high in motivation, self-esteem, confidence and capability. Y people feel empowered and enlightened. They contribute creatively with ideas and initiative. They go that extra mile without anyone needing to ask them to.

> **Theory Y is the culture that you should foster because it operates most effectively. X and Y people are not people who like one style or the other, they are people who have come to feel like this because of the treatment they received.**

Research by Frederick Herzberg prioritised the factors affecting attitudes to work. Achievement, recognition, work, responsibility, advancement and growth were the top six. Money again proved a relative outsider in the ratings, coming more than half way down the 16 factors identified by the research. People who rate money highly are generally missing out in belonging, self expression and fulfilment. See it as your responsibility to change that. How? Help them understand that through achievement rewards come automatically.

Be clear where your major motivational leverage factors are. They are giving a sense of team and personal achievement; giving both team and personal recognition; making the team and personal work enjoyable (and, yes, that means you can have fun!); devolving responsibility and not hugging it all to yourself; and assisting your team members to advance and develop in their personal and professional lives.

Self-motivation exercise 1

How well do you understand what motivates your team members? Make a list for each of them noting their three biggest demotivators. Reflect on how you help to ease or eradicate these issues. Better still, have a discussion with each to see if your assumptions are correct, then talk about how you can both work to ease or eradicate them. Then do the same for yourself.

The secret of 3D motivation

To find the keys to motivating your team members you will need to get to know, understand and appreciate them as human beings. Then, as you learn about each, you will be able to construct an individual motivation profile (IMP) of the different things that "turn on" your different individual team members. Use Herzberg's motivators (achievement, recognition, work, responsibility, advancement and growth) to help you to identify the right amount and type of coaching and mentoring for each team member and build an IMP for each. Also look at them as a group, to enable you to build a picture of the nature and mix of motivational work that you put into your coaching and training for the team.

Self-motivation exercise 2

Write two paragraphs describing yourself as seen by your manager. List three ways you would like to be helped with your motivation. List three things you could do to improve your relationship with your manager. List three things your manager could do to achieve a better relationship with you. Consider your paragraphs and lists, then either take action to work at your own items or, far better, sit down with your manager (or chosen mentor) and discuss your words and both lists.

Use IMPs to plot your course to the perfect motivation mix for all three dimensions: self, team member and team. For each team member you can create a chart on which to monitor your effectiveness. For your team you will then be able to monitor and construct motivational work and activity. And you will also be able to see your own personal needs.

Building IMP charts for your team is easy and fun! Simply get them to carry out the three self-motivation exercises in this chapter and share the results with you! Both of you should keep notes, produce development and action plans and monitor progress together.

Self-motivation exercise 3

List three things you do that irritate your team members. These might be habits or inflexibilities. Then list three things you do that they respect. List the ways you might reduce the first three and increase the second three. Better still, discuss your thoughts with the team in teamwork. Be open, your courage will be respected and admired.

Encourage team members to discuss their IMP with friends, partners, children, and anyone who they admire, or even those who just, as people, simply intrigue or puzzle them. You should do the same with yours. The more you know and understand about yourself and others, the more you know and understand what makes them tick, what gives them a buzz, what excites them – and, therefore, how to encourage, support and motivate them. Don't try to create your team members' IMP without involving them. Let them help you to create the plans that will in turn help them to achieve their goals. Get them to understand what and why you are doing it. Get them to buy in. This, in itself, is a great motivator.

The link between clarity and motivation

High performance sales managers recognise that clarity of the job at hand has a great effect on motivation. If we know what to do and we know how to do it well, our motivation stays high. If we are unclear or have doubts about our task or capability, our motivation will fall.

A key part of being clear about what you have to do is:

- having a clear written job specification, including skills and competences, which is understood;
- having a clear set of procedures which are rehearsed and embedded;
- having a clear set of job standards that are monitored and where performance can be appreciated.

A sales person who feels well managed and assisted towards achievement and success, and who actively feels that his or her skills and competences are being developed, reviewed and reinforced, is a sales team member who has direction, purpose and focus.

1. Motivation has three dimensions: self, team members and team.
2. The Focus Rule of 75: *75% of your time must be spent on motivation.*
3. Motivation is getting people, cheerfully, willingly and professionally to do the things that the business requires them to do.
4. Motivational work will place its major emphasis on the top three layers of the Maslow triangle: belonging, self-expression and self-fulfilment.
5. Understand the XY theory and create a "Y" culture.
6. Achievement, recognition, work, responsibility, advancement and growth are the six prime motivators. Individual Motivation Profiles can be used for individual and team work.
7. Clarity of sales task has a great effect on sales people's motivation.

USING PERFORMANCE TO CREATE WINNERS — Chapter

Coming up in this chapter

OUTcomes and INfluences
Working with Customers
The value of regular visits
Building rapport skills
Prioritising activity
Goal setting

Optimum performance, meaning maximum sales productivity, is achieved through understanding and managing the relationship between what comes out of sales (sales OUTcomes) and what goes into achieving the sales (sales INfluences).

Maximum productivity is reached when the OUTcomes are as high as can be reached and the INfluences are as low as possible. But what are these OUTcomes and INfluences?

○ **OUTcomes** are the results of sales activities: number of sales, number of referrals, revenue, quality of business, mix of products sold, and so on
○ **INfluences** are the number of sales people you have, the nature of the activity they generate, the focus of their time, the number of Customer visits they make, the amount of time on the phone, and so on.

To boost productivity you increase OUTcomes while decreasing INfluences. Can you achieve the same with fewer people? Can you increase the number of Customer visits to increase sales? Can you change a system or process to allow more telephone time for appointment making?

> **"** *The old solution was to chuck resources at the outcomes: more numbers; more this; more that. And it failed. The answer is in managing. By managing we can get the whole team to understand and appreciate that the way to achieve our goals is by working smarter on the INfluences. This automatically provides the desired OUTcomes.* **"**
> **– Derek Hall, Sales Director, LMG plc**

Working with Customers

Customers are your greatest asset and the greatest asset of the business. They deserve looking after to the very best of your team's ability. Here are some thoughts you must consider in order to sustain optimum team performance:

- How well do you know the team territory? How many Customers does your team have in total? How many does each sales person have? Where are they concentrated? Are your resources deployed sensibly?
- Who are your best Customers by spend, by mix of business and by share of wallet? Can you identify the top 100, the top 50, the top 20 and the top 10 Customers handled by your team?
- What can you do to support the sales people in their relationships with these top Customers? Identify the top 10 or even 20 Customers of each sales person and, together, visit those Customers. Let each Customer know how much you appreciate their business. How about a visit just to say "thank you"?

> Don't undermine or usurp the salesperson with your presence and **never** suggest that if a Customer has a problem he or she should come direct to you.

By breeding openness and trust within your team, you will develop an atmosphere between yourself and the team where they will come to respect your advice and experience. Thus when there is an obvious failure to build rapport between one sales person and a Customer or prospect, you can feel free to swap things around to get the best end result for the Customer.

Remembering details about Customers and being able to relate to them knowledgeably are important parts of giving Customers the recognition they deserve. However, the marketing and sales database is the only effective place to capture and hold such information. So, whatever else you do, take a pride in maintaining Customer records and be sure to include lots of information about Customers' circumstances, likes and dislikes, needs, goals, interests and ambitions.

USING PERFORMANCE TO CREATE WINNERS

> **Come at it the other way round**
>
> Try this in a team meeting. Instead of asking what you can do for your Customers, make a list of the things you must not do. Or, to make it more personal, make a list of things you wouldn't like to happen to you if you were a Customer. Examples might be:
>
> ❏ being tricked, deceived or lied to
> ❏ being told only half the story
> ❏ being blinded by science or jargon
> ❏ delays or unreliability
> ❏ not being kept in touch
> ❏ sales people blaming others and not taking personal responsibility
> ❏ being given lame excuses rather than honest answers
> ❏ being patronised or talked down to
>
> Once you have developed your own list then discuss ways to avoid them happening.

You are in control of the balance of INfluences and OUTcomes struck within your team. In order to increase productivity, you should use observation and management of the INfluences to create the maximum OUTcomes.

> " *The last Friday of every month the rep from the paper merchant would spend the whole morning with me. We chatted about new papers, how the paper we had bought ran on the presses, and looked at work we had printed during the month. He kept me in touch with everything to do with paper. For twenty years they've had 85% of our business.* "
> – **J. N. Robinson, Managing Director, Amherst Offset Ltd**

Prioritising time and activity

Sales people perform all manner of contortions to generate "cold" sales activity when it is absolutely, categorically, the most difficult, the most demoralising and the least productive. On the other hand, regular reviews – visiting existing Customers – is always, always, always the most productive. Yet so many sales people ignore it. For this reason we now propose the Customer Rule of 75.

thirty-three

The Customer Rule of 75

Ensure that 75% of all of your team's sales appointments are with existing Customers.

The best way to prioritise sales activity looks like this:

1. Visits to existing Customers/regular reviews
2. Other visits to existing Customers (for example, service calls)
3. Referrals
4. Orphans (previously unassigned Customers)
5. Lapsed Customers
6. Other corporate leads and promotions
7. Cold activities

This next simple three-step process is a high leverage formula. If you don't use it you are quite simply certifiably insane and you should immediately apply for a job as a Kamikaze pilot!

Check the acceptance, understanding and wisdom of the above priority list with your people. It may not have been their personal experience to date but they will find that they are almost instantly more productive when they let this prioritise their activity. The fastest ways to boost their sales effectiveness are as follows:

Step 1: Increase the number of visits to existing Customers
Step 2: Improve their skills with Customer visits.
Step 3: Increase other meaningful contact with Customers (to improve the relationship)

Be quite clear: **THIS WILL GIVE YOU A VERY QUICK UPTURN IN BUSINESS**

Step 1: Increase the number of Customer visits
In order to get the team focused on moving nearer and nearer to the Customer Rule of 75 – to make 75% of your calls to existing Customers – you need to convince them that it's the right thing to

do. Remember, it is 5–15 times easier to re-sell to an existing Customer than to find a new Customer. Make this a priority.

Step 2: Improve their skills with Customer reviews
Since you're moving your team towards a declared aim of making 75% of their calls with existing Customers, it is vital that you also give high priority to building their ability to make these calls valuable and enjoyable to Customers. You have to help them build better, deeper, more important relationships with Customers. In thinking about the work you have to do with and for your team, four main items should get your attention as coaching and training topics.

1. Creating rapport
Communications are vastly improved and more effective when good rapport is created. Good rapport simply means that bodies and words match or echo each other. Only a small percentage of effective communication is to do with the words used. Effective communication comprises 7% verbal (the words used), 38% tone of voice and 55% body influence, such as body language, appearance, posture, gesture and eye contact. Thus, successful rapport helps to make the difference between just verbal contact and truly effective communication. Over 90% of communication is carried out non-verbally. These skills, like verbal skills, can be crafted and tuned by coaching and training.

> " *Rapport enables sales people to be at ease or to put others at ease in a range of situations whether in the home or office. It is, in the widest sense of the word, a social skill. It is also, for a few, a natural and undeveloped skill. For others, it is an unknown or unrecognised facility which can be worked on once awareness has been created and the methods demonstrated.* "
> **– Russell Webster, sales consultant and NLP practitioner**

Both types – the naturally talented and the others – will benefit from rapport work, which should be broken down into readily acquirable components taking them through optimum use of voice (tone, rhythm and speed), eye movements, and body matching. Rapport skills can be used when communicators are both "transmitting" and "receiving"; thus, sales people will be able to observe their Customers' unspoken feelings and desires with more accuracy and will know, for example, when a Customer expresses agreement but his or her heart is not behind the words.

2. Questioning skills
You should develop exercises and drills for the team to show the vague language that people use and how the right question – or, more accurately, framing the question in the right way – can be used to break through barriers. Such skills are ideal for eliciting information, gathering more information, making information more specific or explicit, and finding answers even when clients or prospects don't realise they have one! Getting Customers to feel at ease – feeling they are having a conversation rather than being interrogated – is a core skill.

> **Open and closed questions**
>
> Teach your team the difference between open and closed questions. Open questions uncover Customers' feelings better. Closed questions will lead them to a point:
> - Closed question: *Is that what you want?* They will answer yes or no.
> - Open question: *What do you feel about that?* They can answer any way they feel.

3. Setting specific outcomes
Even those who are accomplished self-goal setters will benefit from the value of being more specific. Setting outcomes can, of course, be used before meetings with Customers, at the beginning of a day, task or project, but, perhaps surprisingly, most usefully it can be used in Customer meetings and shared with the Customer to establish mutual end results and to demonstrate their successful achievement.

Help your team to know precisely the intended result of a meeting; what the Customer wants to achieve (and how to deal with "I don't know" or "I'm not sure"); and how to set and monitor outcomes and know when you've achieved them.

4. Jargon replacement therapy
Although technical terms are necessary in certain key places, it is often more effective to follow the Customer's words than to try to familiarise him or her with the jargon of your business.

Nothing destroys rapport faster than two people speaking different languages! Demonstrate for your team the skills of "word matching" Customers so as not to interfere or distract from the rapport that has been created.

> " *I was selling a convertible term savings plan. The Customer referred to it as Sara's Wedding Day Fund. So that's what we called it from that day on.* "
> **– Karen Rayner, Independent Financial Adviser**

Step 3: Increase regular contact with Customers

It's very difficult to have a good relationship with someone you are going to see, say, just once a year. A Customer might feel neglected by this. Would they automatically pick up the phone to discuss a problem or a worry with an annual visitor? Or would they prefer a friend whose advice they trust?

> **Customers deserve as much contact from your team as possible: a phone call or card on their birthday; a note at Christmas; a visit when you're in the area. They have to see, hear and feel these things and when they experience that it's genuine and for them, the bond is struck. The Quality Lock (see below) is their gift to you. You have their loyalty.**

What skills do you need to have to develop this loyalty? That, of course, will vary from Customer to Customer. Indeed, that is one of the skills: understanding the potential of the relationship. Some will consider a once a year visit to be once too often; others will consider it woefully inadequate.

Building a quality lock
Every business, with even a ghost of a brain cell, is set on a strategy that improves the Customer's lot. This means building Customer satisfaction, creating and managing Customer loyalty and shifting to longer term Customer values. This is to lock

Customers to your businesses and to lock competitors out. An important factor in gaining and maintaining loyalty is "share of wallet", as it is known. The company with the dominant share of that Customer's spend tends to end up being the Customer's favourite choice!

> **TIPS**
>
> The Quality Lock is a method of locking Customers to the business and locking competitors out. Sales people have to create three kinds of trust: trust in the product(s); trust in the company; and trust in themselves as the best source for the product, service or assistance. With these three types of trust robustly developed your Quality Lock is in place.

There is great compatibility between safeguarding Customers from predators and your own need to sell. Do all you can to make sure that your team members realise this and make a conscious choice and effort to spend as near to 75% as possible of their calls with existing Customers.

Guiding your team's development

Don't fall into the trap of becoming an average sales manager. There are two ways to avoid this.

Firstly, constantly remind yourself that the lowest common denominator is just that – the lowest: we're referring to the base standard required by industry regulations, trade associations conditions, ISO 9000, BS 5750, or similar. Low, base and standard are not words associated with high performance.

Secondly, don't let your team feel that they are being checked upon or policed. In financial services, for example, compliance sounds a negative word. Change it. Call it support, assistance, anything that truly reflects the method you are using to cheer your team members on and to help them become the very best sales people they can be.

Prevention is better than cure

In your industry or business the standards are set for you. In your company, the Board set the standards. But in your team, YOU set

USING PERFORMANCE TO CREATE WINNERS

the standards: YOU decide just how good you want your team to be; YOU decide by how much you want to exceed the corporate standards. It's YOUR team and YOUR decision.

1. Optimum performance (maximum sales productivity) is achieved through understanding and managing the relationship between sales OUTcomes and what goes into achieving the sales: sales INfluences.
2. Maximum productivity is reached when the OUTcomes are as high as can be reached by working smarter with the INfluences. OUTcomes are the results of sales activities: INfluences are the things that affect activity and productivity.
3. Who are your best Customers? What can you do to support the sales people in their welding of relationships to these top Customers? Identify the top 20 Customers of each sales person and, together, visit those Customers.
4. The Customer Rule of 75 is that a sales person should ensure that 75% of all appointments are with existing Customers.
5. The order of ease of sale is: visiting existing Customers/ regular reviews; other visits to existing Customers (service calls); family, colleague or other referrals; orphans; lapsed customers. Other leads and cold calling are the lowest priority.
6. The fastest way to boost effectiveness is to: increase the number of regular reviews; improve sales people's skills with reviews; increase contact with Customers. The four areas of importance are: creating rapport; questioning skills; setting specific outcomes; and jargon replacement therapy.
7. Effective communication comprises 7% verbal (the words used), 38% tone of voice and 55% body influence such as body language, posture, gesture and eye contact.
8. Building a Quality Lock is to lock clients to the businesses and to lock competitors out.
9. An important factor in gaining and maintaining loyalty is "share of wallet". To maximise this, sales people have to create three kinds of trust: trust in the product(s); trust in the company; and trust in themselves as the household's or individual's best source of best advice.

The Secrets of Coaching and Training — Chapter 5

Coming up in this chapter

The four stages of learning
Becoming unnecessary – but vital!
Training and coaching methods and topics
Giving and receiving feedback
Accompanied visits
How to become a great leader

Coaching and training – giving guidance and support – are two of your most effective tools to achieve success. A great deal of your motivational work will be done while coaching and training.

Let's look at some basic definitions so that we have a mutual understanding of the words. Training is about the acquisition of skills and coaching is the development of those skills. Therefore both training and coaching should be continuous processes.

Improve your communication, psychological and interpersonal skills and the better the trainer and coach you will become. Many of the skills – for example, building rapport with Customers – may be quite natural to a successful sales person. As a manager you want to develop them further to enhance your power. The fundamental processes of training and coaching are similar. In fact they follow a basic model of learning.

How do we learn?

The learning process has four stages:
- *Stage 1: Unconscious incompetence*
  We are not yet aware that we cannot do something, often because we don't need to. If you are being wheeled around by your mother in a pushchair, you don't need to learn to drive! Stimulated by the need or desire to do it, we reach . . .
- *Stage 2: Conscious incompetence*
  Now we realise what it is we need or desire to do and the fact that we cannot do it. For example, we might say that to get a job in sales, we need to learn to drive.

> While we take lessons and acquire primary skills we go through . . .
> - *Stage 3: Conscious competence*
>   Here we are learning and practising and rehearsing what we have to do. We think about it quite carefully and check how well we're doing everything until it becomes "second nature" to us. We have almost arrived at . . .
> - *Stage 4: Unconscious competence*
>   We are now sufficiently expert at what we do to no longer need to think about it in the same way. We are good at it.

When you learned to drive changing gear was quite difficult. Your instructor first explained that when the engine reaches a certain point, you need to change gear; conscious incompetence. The instructor showed you how to do it, and after a few stalls and shudders, you started to pick it up – but you had to concentrate; conscious competence. Soon you started to be able to change gear quite well, using the rev counter or engine sound; you also started to perfect your knowledge of when to change gear. Finally, you reached the stage where you really didn't pay any attention to the gear change itself, you instinctively knew when to do it, how to do it and which gear to change to; unconscious competence.

Driving is an interesting example to take because it has to be a participative learning process: we subscribe to the following:

I hear	I forget
I see	I remember
I do	I understand

You can and should use participative learning techniques in training work too. Role-play is a good example – one of your team could play the Customer and another the sales person.

> Be sure that you build a virtuous circle between four key elements to make sure that your coaching and training become embedded into your team members' activities. This is the continuous loop created by reviewing, planning, implementation and action.

THE SECRETS OF COACHING AND TRAINING

Think of the sports coach. It helps a coach to have had a good track record in their discipline or sport, but they no longer need to be the best in their team. Their task is to improve their players. Set aside all thoughts of being the best at selling. As a manager, your obsession should be with managing.

Eight top coaching and training attributes

1. Increase your skills in training and coaching.
2. Use your selling skills to get your team's respect and build your credibility.
3. Understand the qualities of leadership (more in this chapter).
4. Appreciate the power of motivation and enthusiasm.
5. Understand the learning process.
6. Develop training programmes.
7. Exchange know-how and ideas with other sales managers.
8. Develop a feeling for your sales people's needs. Build your powers of diagnosis, assessment and development of training programmes.

You should now, quite slowly, read that list of training issues again. And when you have read it again, read it one more time.

- *Use it to prioritise your thinking.*
- *Use it to guide your own development, growth and goal setting.*
- *Use it to determine your own needs and demands for support from your manager.*
- *Use it to build your reading lists.*
- *Use it to plan your conversations with your fellow sales managers.*

YES! The word used in the paragraph at the top of this page was carefully chosen. The eight issues should be your **obsession**.

forty-three

Creating the training and coaching modules

There are four main topics for coaching and training sales teams. You'll find checklists in the TIPS panels throughout this chapter. Add anything else you can think of and set to work. Balance out the things that you know will increase Customer satisfaction and loyalty with the need to sell.

> **Coaching and training topics 1:**
> **The art and craft of professional selling**
>
> - Know-how
> - Identifying Customer needs
> - Product knowledge
> - Use of sales aids
> - Use of events (awards, ad campaigns, PR, current news)
> - Handling objections
> - Listening
> - Advising
> - Creating rapport
> - Use of questions (open, closed, and so on)
> - Use of a laptop computer as a sales aid (if appropriate)
> - Approach to Customers
> - Approach to prospects
> - Opening
> - Obtaining Referrals
> - Closing
> - Telephone technique
> - Written communication skills
> - Turning features into benefits
> - Creativity and ideas generation
> - Decision making

Giving and receiving feedback

Inevitably, an element of your feedback will be critical or negative. Even negative feedback can, and should, be given in a helpful and positive way. However, there are some ground rules for giving feedback. Use JFR's Nine Golden Rules of Feedback and you will find your communications are clearer and better received, even when they are negative.

1. Always give feedback as quickly as possible after an event.
2. Never criticise the person. Criticise the behaviour or process. For example, "Only an idiot would do it like that!" should be "That's not the best way to do that" or, better still, "Do you think there might be a better way to do that?"

3. Always remind team members before feedback that the aim is positive – you are doing your best to help their development and growth.
4. Make all criticism accurate, factual and specific.
5. Give criticism openly by stating your feelings and take responsibility for them. Then ask the team members' views. Listen. Be prepared to debate.
6. Never let tempers become involved. If they should, restore calm before continuing.
7. Ask for feedback for yourself; for example, "How do you feel I handled that?" or "Have you any suggestions to help me improve that?"
8. Do everything in your power to give negative feedback in a way that leaves the team member feeling valued and appreciated.
9. Always, ALWAYS, **ALWAYS, ALWAYS** begin and end in a positive manner.

Giving negative feedback

- Tell things as you perceived them.
- Describe the negative behaviour or practice specifically and avoid being judgmental.
- Describe and seek agreement on an outcome: an undesirable outcome is the continuation of the negative behaviour or process.
- Seek the view of the person receiving the criticism.
- Agree and gain commitment to a negotiated behavioural change.

We all love recognition, praise and approval. You'll find the same is true with your team members.

**Coaching and training topics 2:
Working on individuals (and yourself!)**

- Team spirit
- Enthusiasm
- Confidence
- Self-motivation
- Positive attitude
- Warm and friendly disposition
- Energy
- Presentation and health
- Empathy
- Stress management
- Time management

Preparation for an accompanied visit

A lot of coaching will revolve around accompanied visits and require careful planning. Don't carry out coaching sessions combined with appraisals. You cannot do justice to either the coaching or the appraisal if they are undertaken at the same time, and it can create confusing messages for the team member.

The planning and role-sharing discussions for accompanied visits fall into three stages: before, during and after. Many sales managers cover preparation with a quick phone call, attend the visit and dash off soon afterwards promising "I'll call you". This is no way to manage and no way to coach. High performance sales managers learn to value their time with team members immediately prior to, and immediately following, a call.

Use the checklist (contained in the ACT boxes) prior to an accompanied call. It starts with pre-call activity (what you must do to bring yourself up to speed with what happened during and since the last meeting with the prospect or Customer):

Preparation checklist: pre-call

- ❑ Background: date of sales person's last visit; needs/products discussed at that meeting, if any; objections raised; review and discuss all Client information.
- ❑ Planning: call objectives; any known Customer needs; product knowledge; sales aids to be used; information or details to be given to Customer; introductions and call opening; need – product – benefit matching (see below); questions to be asked; answers or information needed; most likely objections and handling of them; any role-play rehearsals required; call closing ideas; agree the part you will take.

"Need – product – benefit matching" is a key component of sales integrity and is also a major component in the sales case. Many successful sales people like to go through a process of seeking out the "need behind the need", believing that in this way you uncover deeper reasons in the Customer for buying from you and often the Customer then overcomes his or her objections.

For example, we have a friend who has very adequate pension arrangements. Asked why, he said, "I want to make sure my retirement is comfortable, of course". Asked why, he paused, reflected and then said, "Because I watched my parents have a really hard time coping on the state pension together with an awfully inadequate scheme Dad had from work. And, in those days there wasn't much I could do to help financially speaking. I wouldn't want my children to have to watch me, helpless to do anything simply because I didn't think it through now."

Our friend's real need was to avoid causing his children the same guilt and anxiety he had suffered watching his own parents struggle. And, yes, it gave him a comfortable retirement into the bargain. The need behind the need was uncovered simply with two open questions: "Why?" and "Why?" Asking them is easy. Creating the rapport, trust and openness with someone who is a Customer and not necessarily a friend is the real skill! Once created, it will shatter like fragile glass the moment you abuse it.

> **Preparation checklist: during the call**
>
> ❏ Observation and assessment: stay connected with the team member; avoid being drawn in by the Customer; make enough contact to maintain courtesy; avoid intervening, rescuing and taking over; check call path against plan; note validity and effect of diversions from plan; SWOT the presentation (see below); note whether objectives were achieved; note progress since last accompanied call; note areas for improvement; note everything being done well.

"SWOT" stands for strengths, weaknesses, opportunities and threats. It is a widely used system of situational or competitive analysis. In its simplest form it is very easy to use. On a sheet of paper or flipchart, draw a cross dividing the page into four. From the top left, clockwise, head each section Strengths, Weaknesses, Opportunities and Threats, and then review the situation. No item should be entered in more than one category. Once complete you have a list of those things that need attention.

Use SWOT analysis with your team as a problem solving exercise. It's a great start to a planning session!

> **Preparation checklist: after the call**
>
> ❏ Feedback: praise everything done well in detail; use open questioning to lead and coax critical self-analysis; use reversed role play – they play the Customer, you the sales person; agree the follow-up and self-learning priorities; discuss when repetition possibilities may occur; identify and gain acceptance and agreement to further coaching and training needs; set objectives for the next accompanied call; agree the timing of a review of issues raised; close with a highlighted summary of what was done well.

How to become a great leader

> " *Of a great leader, the people will say, 'we did it ourselves'.* "
> – **Lao Tzu**

This is a fundamental key learning point for team leaders. They need to understand that their true aim is to enable their team members to "do it themselves". When your sales people can do it themselves they will be able to get in front of Customers being and feeling really confident, supremely competent and knowledgeable. It is hard to learn, but truly important to know, when to intervene and you must never interfere. Appreciate that, as a leader, your task is to serve, nurture and cultivate those who are doing the real work of the business.

> " *As leader of a team, my aim was to reach a point where, in terms of the day-to-day work of the team, I was unnecessary – yet absolutely vital. For the process and content of their routine work, my team functioned without me. However, for their motivation, energy, enthusiasm and spirit, they really needed me.* "
> – **Abraham Gooding, National Sales Manager, Cool Gourmet Catering**

During most stages of the Customer relationship, the sales people are predominantly the ones involved. Sales management is there to enable, empower and develop them to be able to perform to the very best of their ability. Senior management are there to provide exactly the same assistance to the sales management. This is a "win–win" process.

THE SECRETS OF COACHING AND TRAINING

> **Coaching and training topics 3:**
> **commitment to organisation and administration**
>
> - Tidiness
> - Condition of sales aids
> - Internal communications
> - Administration issues
> - Keeping promises
> - State of car
> - The open briefcase (impression made by!)
> - Record keeping
> - Time keeping
> - Appointment making
> - Appointment keeping

The manager as leader

As a manager, you are, first and foremost, a leader. Your greatest resource is your team. You must value and nurture them. If you lead them well, you will achieve. Treat them exactly as you would have them treat their Customers and prospects.

Leadership is about helping others to realise their own potential – empowerment. Add to that the strength, power and commitment that being part of a well-led team brings to people and you will have understood a critical part of your role as a high performance sales manager.

People get a buzz out of being respected, praised, trusted and admired. Through leading and coaching, team members feel the difference: they feel encouraged rather than criticised; they feel supported rather than denigrated; they feel they are being cultivated rather than victimised. All these add to their motivation.

> **Coaching and training topics 4:**
> **making the most of time and work**
>
> - Goal setting
> - Preparation and planning
> - Call rate
> - Conversion rate
> - Sales values
> - Use of leads, etc.
> - Client reviews or other issues
> - Openness
> - Relationship building
> - Pre-call planning and preparation
> - Day activity planning
> - Journey planning
> - Commitment to and involvement with coaching and training

So, what is the meaning of all this to your coaching and training work? Quite simply, less is more. In other words, your task is not to be on your feet all day spouting about how the team must do things. It is much, much more about enabling them openly to discuss their successes and failures. See their failures as opportunities; opportunities for them to grow and develop. There is no failure to a good team leader; only feedback. Use feedback to help you and your team adjust what you do. Feedback is the great learning opportunity to decide what to do next and differently. Failure is when the same thing goes wrong a second time.

TIPS

1. Remember the Four Stages of Learning: unconscious incompetence; conscious incompetence; conscious competence; unconscious competence. Remember also, I hear – I forget; I see – I remember; I do – I understand.
2. Developing learning programmes needs creativity and ideas. Make sure these programmes involve the team. The top teaching and training attributes are to be found in: increasing your management and communication skills; using selling skills to get the team behind you and build your credibility; understanding the qualities of leadership; appreciating the power of motivation and enthusiasm; and creating an environment which respects and honours growth and learning.
3. There are four main topics for coaching and training sales teams: the art and craft of professional selling; working on oneself; commitment to organisation and administration; making the most of time and work.
4. Giving and receiving feedback should be tackled as quickly as possible after the event; criticise the process or behaviour, not the person; give negative feedback so that the team member feels valued and appreciated; begin and end positively.
5. As a manager, you are, first and foremost, a leader. Your greatest resource is your team. Leadership is about helping others to realise their fullest potential.

RUNNING GREAT SALES TEAM MEETINGS — Chapter 6

Coming up in this chapter...

Where to get help
Beginnings, middles and ends
A CLEAR formula for successful meetings
Before you meet
Checklist for great meetings

Behind all great meetings is great planning

It is not necessarily hard work to create memorable, motivational and effective meetings, but it does need thought, planning and preparation. Think of it as producing a play or film. Each scene – or, for your meetings, topic – needs working out: the cast, the role they will play, the script and the props and location.

Becoming a good leader of sales meetings

There are three places where you should expect help with the skills required to lead effective sales team meetings. One is right here – the remainder of this chapter. The second is your peer group.

Get together with other sales managers. Compare notes. Discuss your progress and your problems. Exchange ideas and successes. Exchange your failures too, as this stops you and others from making the same mistakes. If one particular manager is doing better than you, don't just sit there wrapped in envy, dismay and ignorance. Ask how he or she does it. If you have found something that works exceedingly well and you know another manager is having problems, don't just sit there smug and pious. Offer to help. If the things improve, the Customer wins. If the Customer wins, we all win. It's a mutual process.

The third place you should expect support, guidance and help is from your manager. You are not being asked to give anything to your team you shouldn't get yourself. If you think your team meeting skills need sharpening, ask for help. Your manager should be acting as a catalyst to help all the teams improve. While you may be seeking peer group support, your team leader should also be offering it. And you, too, should be experiencing just the kind of team spirit that you are creating around yourself. If it is not happening, SHOUT.

Thinking it through

Before getting into meeting content, here are a few tips to keep meetings positive, alive and enjoyable.

Meetings need orchestration. They have a beginning, a middle (usually the core segment) and an end. Each of these needs thought and attention, which is another mark of the high performance sales manager. Yet many managers create an agenda, plonk it in front of people and wait to see what happens.

Regular as clockwork?

Meetings often become boring and pointless simply because they are regular. This is not to say periodic or regular meetings are wrong, but on the occasions when there is less to fill them, it is sometimes better to delay them until there is sufficient content. One thing is certain, late morning starts and early afternoon finishes lead to poor productivity. These are not the signs of a highly motivated team bursting with ideas and energy. They are the signs of a bored, demotivated team who are more anxious to get home to the TV. Choose your day – a day that you can fill, and do just that!

If you can get some matters resolved over the phone, by mail, e-mail, or fax, then do it. But remember, you can't build team spirit over the phone and you can't deal with team motivation individually.

Consider why many meetings turn out to be either a brilliant, productive, highly motivating experience or a dismal, diabolical, time-wasting drag. For the main part, it is your leadership and stewardship that will make the pendulum swing one way or the other.

The power and energy of the group as a whole makes things work, building team motivation, morale and commitment. If a key player or a number of people are going to be missing, it is better to have a delayed meeting than a bad one.

> **Before you meet**
>
> - Plan your meeting. What will you do for a beginning, middle and ending?
> - Phone round in advance to build your agenda.
> - Make sure you include team members' issues as well as your own on the agenda.
> - Always start meetings by going round the group to agree desired outcomes for the day. Don't forget yours!
> - Always include some element of training, motivation and a team exercise.
> - Plan your agenda to finish meetings on time.

As team leader you must be disciplined. If you find that you are becoming over-involved with one member, on one issue, note it and agree to finish the discussion elsewhere at a later time, such as immediately after the meeting. No single member or member's issue should dominate or claim more than a fair share of time.

> Never worry about saying "We'll give this three more minutes and then we're moving on" to retain focus and maintain your purpose for the day.

Always close meetings with a summary of the main points. Backtrack through the proceedings and check for agreement and consensus. Re-run any allocation of tasks and projects. Re-confirm any timings or demands.

Checklist for a great meeting

Here's a checklist for you to work with. Some are things to do, some are things to remember, some are things to think about.

1. *Explain the events briefly at the beginning. Everyone likes to know what's going to happen, what the timings are, and what*

is expected of them by way of contribution. Avoid surprises . . . unless they are very, very good surprises.
2. Ring round and pre-brief the team on the objectives; discuss any thoughts or contributions they might make; tell them if you have any requirements of them.
3. Do everything you can to make group decisions. Lead, don't command!
4. Always recap and summarise before moving on. And then do it again at the end.
5. Involve weaker members of the team and exercise control over the stronger ones.
6. Discourage stronger members from – and if necessary penalise them for – talking over weaker ones. Ensure that one person speaks at a time. Stay focused on the agenda and outcomes.
7. Avoid becoming the preacher. If you spend all day on your feet spouting it will be thoroughly demotivating (however good you are). Let the days be full of discussion, debate, involvement, activity and participation.
8. If you have any standard or regular information or figures to distribute, circulate them in advance. This gives the team time to think about them and discussion will improve. If anyone seems not to have studied them, let them know why you pre-circulate them!
9. Consider rotating the chair. If you decide to chair, remember to stay neutral during discussions. You're allowed a view, of course, but it shouldn't prevail because you are in the chair!
10. Always include a team motivation exercise or training element
11. Use the meeting to discuss, resolve or find alternative solutions to team concerns and problems – or even your own work issues.

A formula for effective meetings

Effective sales meetings need a CLEAR formula: Cocktail; Lively; Enthusiasm; Ask, don't tell; Record.

- **Cocktail:** vary the pattern, proceedings and content of your meetings. Why should one meeting be like the previous one . . . or the next one? DULL! Use a range of different techniques, a blend of various styles and a mix of topics.
- **Lively:** keep meetings lively and entertaining. Topics should be kept short. Keep the pace up and the action going.

- ❑ **Enthusiasm:** remember just how much of the motivational process should come from sales meetings. Do positive things to build enthusiasm. Remember, it's catching. But they won't catch it unless you've got it first.
- ❑ **Ask, don't tell:** this style increases involvement and participation. It also keeps people connected, alert and stimulated.
- ❑ **Record:** in order to encourage the generation of ideas and to demonstrate that you welcome and respect them, make sure you record all ideas using a flipchart. Mark the initials of the originator alongside. After the meeting, circulate them (with the initials, in other words, credits, still in place).

However, celebrating and recording the great ideas is pointless unless you do something positive to action or implement them.

The Action Rule of 75

Many, many sales meetings spend too much time picking over the boring old bones of the past. You can't change history – although you can learn from it. So set agendas for your meetings that adhere to . . .

> **The Action Rule of 75**
>
> Spend 75% of sales meetings working on the future.

You should spend some time dealing with, reflecting on, analysing or even announcing results. However, they are history. The past. They've gone. The future is what counts. If you limit the past to 25%, today onwards will get 75% and that's the way it should be. And plenty of that time should be spent in action planning.

fifty-five

TIPS

1. Meetings need planning to be memorable, motivational and effective.
2. Meetings need orchestration. They have a beginning, a middle (usually the core segment) and an end. Each of these three needs thought and attention.
3. Set agenda and plan to include team and your own issues – and to finish on time.
4. It is important to have a CLEAR formula.
5. The Action Rule of 75: **spend 75% of sales meetings working on the future.**
6. Always include motivational team exercises and training.

READY FOR LIFT-OFF
Chapter 7

Coming up in this chapter

If you go on doing . . .
Get ready now!
Celebrate your power
An open door to success

Change is not an option

As a sales manager you must take notice that you are in a time of change. Change from the old "command and control" culture to the new "empowered and responsible" culture. For sales people, and especially sales managers, it can be quite difficult to stop a habit or routine. They experience what works and make it a routine. The older they get, or perhaps the longer they go on getting results with something, the more "right" it feels to them.

Often, when discussing change or transformation projects, I use the following well-worn saying:

> **If you go on doing what you've always done, you will go on getting what you always got. If it's not working, CHANGE IT!**

The trouble with change is that we all have to stop doing what we know how to do and start doing something we don't know how to do, at least not yet. This is why the favourite human reaction to change is that we relate the problems of the present to the solutions of the past. Now, suddenly, they no longer fit. If you are new to sales management, this could equally be true of the change you must make from selling to managing.

Why wait for a crisis? Get ready now!

One of the recent management "discoveries" is that, given the opportunity, freedom and encouragement, people will perform better than they will if given a tight corset of rules, instructions and discipline. It's known as "tight/loose controls". It means your targets are clear and precise – tight; but how you achieve them is up to you – loose. It empowers people to be managed this way and that is the very power that it unleashes in them. That self same power is what you want to foster, develop and set free within your team; the power to achieve and excel and to feel you did it yourself. It is YOUR power.

This can only be achieved if you commit to it unreservedly. If you have doubts and fears about it, discuss them with your colleagues, your team and your manager. Don't ever bury or dismiss doubt. It will hold back high performance. Your motivation will sag. Your work will suffer. By embracing change, the reverse will happen. When you believe in it, trust it and commit yourself to it, then change is less painful and you develop through it. You energise yourself. You eventually realise that you can do it. And your belief in yourself once again becomes strong and robust.

Self-assessment check up

This is another exercise you can do on your own, if you so choose; then as you feel it becomes appropriate, do it with your team and discuss their assessment of you. You may already feel comfortable about it, in which case put it straight into teamwork. This table is a simple questionnaire. Score yourself out of 5: if you find you agree entirely with the statement or that it is already part of your team structure, give yourself 5; if you find you disagree or don't want it to be part of your team structure, give yourself 1. *You must be honest with yourself!*

I truly care about my team, and they feel and know it	1 2 3 4 5
I appraise and assess performance more regularly than other managers	1 2 3 4 5
I always take feedback after coaching, training and observed activity	1 2 3 4 5
All our goal setting – as individuals and as a team – is done together	1 2 3 4 5
My staff respect me and I find this works better than fear and discipline	1 2 3 4 5
I know my team as individuals and I know how they differ in skills	1 2 3 4 5
I have looked at motivation on an individual basis and talked about it with each of them	1 2 3 4 5
I never find that I have to tell them what to do and we talk and work it out together	1 2 3 4 5
As a team, we always try to make decisions together and this way works better	1 2 3 4 5

I make a point of knowing the personal needs of my team members	1 2 3 4 5
I am always anxious to improve my management skills and my team help me	1 2 3 4 5
I do not have a problem with my attitude to the company; it's always positive	1 2 3 4 5
When my team are at their best, they simply have to generate enough acitivity to win	1 2 3 4 5
My team meetings are interesting, fun, involve the whole team and build motivation	1 2 3 4 5
The team and I have developed a training plan based on their needs as a unit	1 2 3 4 5
I feel supported by my manager and know that I can ask for help at any time	1 2 3 4 5
At team meetings we avoid sarcasm and negativity as they are not helpful	1 2 3 4 5
Team spirit is something we all value and work at and we like helping each other	1 2 3 4 5
I am liked and admired by my team	1 2 3 4 5

Grade yourself. Be soul-baringly honest. Use this exercise to uncover and help with the planning of your own development. You should certainly discuss this with your own manager. Get him or her to agree with you a plan of coaching and training to meet your own needs.

The maximum score is 100. If you score over 75, apply for the Sales Director's job now; over 85, check it with your team today; over 95, and you have a God-like status. You are also kidding yourself!

Seven tips for the high performer

1. *Constantly review your time management. Put real energy into organising yourself to have as much teamtime as possible and to minimise your officework time.*
2. *Become a master of feedback. Safe, sincere and deep feedback – giving and receiving – is a craft. Learn it. Work at it. You will develop a closeness and intimacy with your team which is incredibly powerful.*
3. *Coach and train at every possible opportunity. Make people*

aware of their successes and build their motivation. Create a team atmosphere of personal growth and development. Let learning be celebrated!
4. The Customer should come first. Encourage your team to prioritise their activity with existing Customers right at the top of the list.
5. When you are considering motivation, don't underestimate the power of clarity of purpose. Remember these words: "If I know what to do and I know how to do it well, my motivation stays high; if I am unclear or have doubts about my task or capability, my motivation will fall".
6. Before you decide anything, ask yourself: is this good or bad for our motivation? When a negative answer rears its ugly head, find the positive motivational way to approach and overcome it. That is really managing!
7. Take yourself seriously. Look at the skills that made you a brilliant sales person. Use them to develop and improve your team. Look at the areas where you failed; welcome the identification of failure or weakness for what it is, and vigorously set about changing it. Let the whole world help with this: your team; your manager; your partner, husband or wife; your friends and family. Even your Customers will feed back to you, as long as you make it a comfortable, enjoyable and happy experience for them. To learn most of what you have to learn, learn to put this last tip first.

> Now you must be uncompromising. Together with your team simply ask the following checklist of 28 questions over the course of your next sales meetings. Pick a couple at a time. There are always means, methods and paths to improvement, so continue asking them. It's a continuous process. There's no such thing as a perfect sales manager and no such thing as a perfect sales person!

The 28 key questions that drive high performance

1. How could we better satisfy all our Customer needs?
2. How could we better serve our Customers?
3. Is our motivation as high as it has ever been?
4. Is motivation rising or falling generally?
5. How does the corporate and/or team mission statement connect to motivation?
6. Are each sales person's individual motivations understood and acted upon?

7. As a team, how could we improve our motivation work?
8. How could we make our sales team meetings more motivational?
9. How can we help each other to increase enthusiasm?
10. How could we improve our agenda setting, meeting reviews and feedback?
11. How can we increase the amount of training time we spend in sales meetings?
12. How can we increase the amount of action planning we do at sales meetings?
13. Could our training and coaching plans be more explicit, clearer, better planned and kept on track?
14. Have we done all we could to build a self-improvement culture – for example, a team library of videos, tapes and books?
15. Have we perfected our use of performance analysis and management reports for diagnosis of coaching and training?
16. How could we improve the way appraisals are carried out?
17. What would improve our giving and receiving of feedback?
18. How can we be more open with and supportive of team members?
19. How can we decrease poor sales performance and increase effectiveness?
20. How can we find more time to coach and train?
21. Is the training and development programme a product of team debate and decision making?
22. Is the training programme clearly published and adhered to?
23. What more can we do to increase Customer satisfaction and loyalty?
24. What extra thing can we do each day to bring one more referral, one more presentation and one more sale?
25. Do we know what to do with complaints and how to get the best resolutions?
26. How could we improve our liaison with other internal departments to help the Customer get a quicker, more accurate response?
27. How can we increase our team spirit?
28. How can we help each other to improve our core sales skills?

" Always give 100%. If we could get by on 99.9%, there would be two unsafe landings at Chicago's O'Hare airport every day! "
– Sid Friedman, for 17 consecutive years the most successful insurance salesman in the USA

HIGH PERFORMANCE SALES MANAGEMENT

How will you know when you've become a high performance manager?

For a start, life will be hectic but happy and fulfilling. Your self-esteem and confidence will be high – possibly the highest they have ever been. And it is quite possible that your personal, as well as business, relationships will have improved substantially.

> **TIPS**
> - High performers understand the value of relationships.
> - High performers know that relationships have to be worked at.
> - High performers put the relationship before the sale, knowing that plenty of sales will come from enough well-managed and successful Customer relationships.

One of the ways in which you will know whether you have achieved high performance is that you will really become aware of your own growth and development. Your results will show it too – both your sales results and your assessment and appraisal results.

Achieving high performance benefits your Customers, your work and working relationships, it benefits your loved ones and it benefits you. Achieving high performance is a wise goal. It is a commendable place to be for your career. But most of all, it is a set of skills, human qualities and characteristics of which you can be truly proud.

And finally . . .

Thank you for your time and attention. We truly hope that, even if it is only in some small way, this book adds to your life and work. But we would hope that it might do so in a big way.

This book is part of the JFR's Essential Secrets series. We're tackling all sorts of sales, marketing and other business issues. Forthcoming are books on making meetings work, working from home, speaking in public, and so on. Hopefully, you'll collect those that are relevant for you and keep your eye out for the new ones as they are published. If you would like to send feedback please e-mail us at jfr@jfr.co.uk. To join our mailing list simply leave your address there.

READY FOR LIFT-OFF

1. If you go on doing what you've always done, you will go on getting what you always got. If it's not working, **CHANGE IT!**
2. Given the opportunity, freedom and encouragement, people will perform better – it empowers them. Foster, develop and set free this power within your team. The power to achieve and excel; and to feel you did it yourself. It is YOUR power.
3. The seven best tips for your path to high performance are:
   - constantly review your time management
   - become a master of feedback
   - coach and train at every possible opportunity
   - understand the cultural change that is taking place
   - don't underestimate the power of clarity of purpose
   - ask yourself: is this good or bad for our motivation?
   - take yourself seriously – and to learn most of what you have to learn, learn to put this last tip first.
4. How will you know when you've become a high performance manager? Your life will be hectic, happy and fulfilling. Your self-esteem and confidence will be high. Personal and business relationships will be improved substantially. High performers understand the value of relationships. High performers know that relationships have to be worked at. High performers put the relationship before the sale, knowing that sales will come from enough successful Customer relationships.
5. Remember the five Rules of 75 for high performance sales managers:
   - The Golden Rule of 75: when you have captured at least 75% of the Customers' available spend, you know you have secured their trust, their loyalty and their affection.
   - The Time Rule of 75: organise your time and activities to enable you to spend 75% of your time out with your team.
   - The Focus Rule of 75: of all the time that you spend with your team 75% of your time must be spent on motivation.
   - The Customer Rule of 75: ensure that 75% of all appointments are with existing Customers.
   - The Action Rule of 75: spend 75% of sales meetings working on the future.

Forthcoming titles in this series will include

- *Winning Sales Letters*
- *Win–Win Negotiation*
- *How to Wow and Audience*
- *Make the Most of Meetings*
- *Key Account Management*
- *Coping with Company Politics*
- *Winning CVs*
- *How to Pay Less Tax*

Do you have ideas for subjects which could be included in this exciting and innovative series? Could your company benefit from close involvement with a forthcoming title?

Please contact David Grant Publishing Limited
80 Ridgeway, Pembury, Tunbridge Wells, Kent TN2 4EZ
Tel/Fax +44 (0)1892 822886
Email GRANTPUB@aol.com
with your ideas or suggestions.